Contents

Before Approaching the Podium

I. The Three Rules of Public Speaking 3

    Rule #1: Keep It Simple. 3

    Rule #2: Repetition Is Good. Repetition Is Good. 4

    Rule #3: Be Prepared! 6

II. Writing the Talk 7

    Types of Talks 8

    What's the Takeaway? 10

    Your Audience 11

    Writing the Talk 12

    Signposts 15

    Avoiding Plagiarism 17

    How Do You Document Sources? 18

III. Presenting the Talk 19

    Practice, practice, practice 19

    Use Your Voice 20

    What about Stage Fright? 20

    What about Visual Aids? 21

    Final Reminders 25

Words and Phrases to Avoid (or Use Sparingly) 26

A Rubric for Evaluating a Talk 28

Acknowledgments / Works Cited 29

Before Approaching the Podium

This little book is intended as a succinct, accessible, and visually inviting undergraduate introduction to the essentials of public speaking. It is for students in any first- or second-year college course requiring presentations, like English Composition.

SPEAK: How to Talk to Classmates and Others is something like your first bicycle. It's not fancy, but if you learn its lessons, then you can ride off and give an effective talk at school, at work, or in the community.

Here are public speaking essentials, which you can call on forever and, like riding a bike, you'll *never forget.*

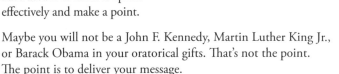

SPEAK first came to be in 2008 as part of the SAGES program at Case Western Reserve University. Since then, over 4,000 students taking seminars on a variety of topics have used it to learn to speak effectively and make a point.

Maybe you will not be a John F. Kennedy, Martin Luther King Jr., or Barack Obama in your oratorical gifts. That's not the point. The point is to deliver your message.

So—on to Rule #1 of oral presentations …

I. The Three Rules of Public Speaking

Every talk has a key message.
If this primer were a talk, its key message would be:
There are three cardinal rules for giving oral presentations.

Rule #1: Keep It Simple.

Your audience may consist of the most intelligent, well-informed, and attentive listeners you could hope for. Still, as they listen to your talk, they are operating under several disadvantages:

> They can't highlight it.
>
> They can't thumb through it later.
>
> They can't <u>underline</u> what they hear you say.
>
> They can't *jot down* marginal notes on your talking.

All they have is what they hear.

For this reason, your topic, message, and argument must be stated in words, phrases, and examples that are

Clear
Direct
Easy to remember

NOT: *"Your thesis, or message, or whatever you might call the most important point you want your listeners to remember, and which will be the topic sentence from which your main argument, and its various sub-arguments, will flow in a deductive and quite syllogistical manner, has to be written in a way that they are sure to recall, even after you have said it in several different ways."*

Huh? (And no one's impressed.)

Remember, too, that simplicity does not come easily. You may have to rewrite your key message two dozen times before you get it right.

> You're on an elevator on the 17th floor with a casual acquaintance. The door closes, the elevator descends for the 20-second ride down, and she asks: "So, what's your talk about?" If you can tell her your subject, objective, and message before the door opens, without speed-talking, you win!

Rule #2: Repetition Is Good.
Rule #2: Repetition Is Good.

Here's the oldest rule of speechmaking:

> First, tell them what you are going to tell them.
> Then, tell them.
> Then, tell them what you told them.

In other words, repetition of your key message is good. (Get that? Repeating your key message is o.k.) Although this rule may not apply to other forms of communication, it definitely applies to oral presentations.

Repetition is good because your audience consists of listeners, not readers. Listeners need to be reminded what your message is, because they can't flip back to the beginning and review it for themselves. They need to hear it expressed in different words, because they may not understand it the first time. And, hard as it may be to believe, they need to hear the message again and again because their minds may wander.

The "Tell them . . . tell them . . . tell them" pattern gives you a handy framework for your presentation.

An **INTRODUCTION** tells your listeners what you are going to tell them:

> "I want to talk today about . . ."

> "My talk today concerns some research findings about . . ."

The **ARGUMENT** tells them:

> "A second group of studies confirms the point
>   I have been making . . ."

> "Recent discoveries are consistent with the view that . . ."

And the **CONCLUSION** tells them what you told them:

> "As we have seen . . ."

> "For all the reasons I have stated, the government
>   is justified in . . ."

The conclusion gives closure. It completes the circle, taking the listeners back to the beginning of your talk. As they say in the business world, repeating your core message gives your listeners the "takeaway" you want them to remember when they leave the room.

introduction ▸ argument ▸ conclusion

Rule #3: Be Prepared!

Know your stuff cold. The better you know your material, the more engaging and interesting you will be, and the less anxious you will feel. You will also be more in control, able to take questions in stride, answer them, and not get thrown off track.

> Bring notes, in whatever form you find most comfortable (index cards, a yellow pad). You can even prepare a script, if the act of writing helps you learn the material.
>
> BUT DO NOT READ FROM IT.   (BORING!)

In sum:

SIMPLICITY   **REPETITION**   **PREPARATION**

These are the three cardinal rules—and the main message of this chapter (repeated one more time).[2]

Now, let's build your talk . . .

[DON'T 👂 FORGET]

---

[1] **P.S. Why only three rules?** You could say there are six, eight, or ten key rules.
But people easily remember three, no more than five. Make it easy for a listener to remember.

II. Writing the Talk

The secret to being a bore is to tell everything.

—*Voltaire*

Voltaire at 70. Engraving from 1843 edition of his *Philosophical Dictionary*.

Voltaire is right. Plus, the more you say, the less people remember. Recall **Rule #1**: Keep it simple and easy to remember. Of all the interesting, important, impressive, funny, weird things you could say about your research, **what is the fundamental message you want to convey? What's the takeaway?** That question is the guiding star by which you navigate your way through the writing process.

Types of Talks

Why are you giving this talk?
Depending on your purpose, you may be delivering:

An Informative Speech
A speech that imparts **knowledge** about a topic (why the U.S. withdrew from Vietnam, how voice-recognition software works) or explains how to do something (dance the tango, bake a pizza).

A Persuasive Speech
The classic **making-a-case** argument speech (why your audience should support—or oppose—gun control or the expansion of Medicaid, why lottery tickets are a poor investment).

A Special Occasion Speech
Anything from a ceremonial **wedding** toast to a speaker **introduction**, from **remarks** at a recognition ceremony or memorial service to a **pep talk**.

Classifying your speech—understanding its rhetorical purpose—helps you direct your thinking and channel your creative work in crafting your talk.

staff reports   proposals

thesis defenses   pep talks

academic papers

wedding toasts
business pitches

welcoming a speaker   selling yourself

press conferences

Talks are different from papers . . .
You are more **CONSTRAINED** than in a paper.

> A talk is **shorter**.
> Its **topic appeals to your audience** *(not just your professor).*[1]
>
> Your choice of **facts and events must be attuned** to your audience.
> *Will your deep technical knowledge of filming horror*
> *movies go over the heads of your listeners?*
>
> You must **look and sound convincing**
> *(unlike you at 4 a.m. as you email in your beautifully*
> *formatted paper).*

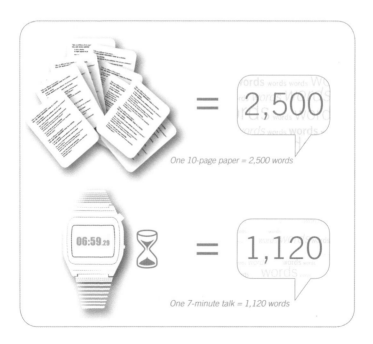

One 10-page paper = 2,500 words

One 7-minute talk = 1,120 words

[2] See Your Audience, p. 11 and Ethos, p. 14.

What's the Takeaway?

Your purpose in giving an oral presentation is to make a difference in your audience's awareness, knowledge, or understanding of your subject. **Everything you include in your oral presentation must contribute to the key message you want your audience to take away from your talk.**

"Takeaway" is not to be confused with "Take Out."

Here are two tips to get your writing started:

State your key message in one short sentence.
This can be a challenge. But once you distill your message into a simple statement **(Rule #1)**, you will have an easier time repeating it throughout the talk **(Rule #2)** and rehearsing **(Rule #3)**.

Write an outline.
An outline is a good way to get your thoughts in order and give yourself a roadmap, even if it's a rough one. The act of writing will pump your thinking.

Some speakers like a formal outline (I. A. 1. (a), etc.); others jot down ideas in a more casual format. Different styles fit different writers, but in every case your outline will evolve and shift as you decide how best to get your message across.

If you follow the "Tell them what you are going to tell them" principle, your outline may look something like this:

- Introduction [the preview]
  - Significance or importance of the topic
  - Background or context
- The argument [telling them] (carefully selected facts, figures, quotes that explain and support your argument)
- Summary [tell them what you told them] and conclusion

There are several other possible organizing principles as well:

① Chronological order

  ② Cause and effect

    ③ Numerical order

      ④ Problem-solution approach

        ⑤ Geographical order

          ⑥ Alphabetical order

            ⑦ Psychological order

But don't forget to "Tell them what you are going to tell them; tell them; tell them what you told them."

Your Audience

Always consider your listeners as you write.

Be sensitive to:

Their knowledge of the subject matter and technical terms

Their preconceived notions about the topic

Their age

Their educational level

Also consider the institutional context. Are you speaking to a diverse audience, with varied interests and perspectives? Or do your listeners share a common lingo, acronyms, and work culture?

Remember: your audience for an oral presentation in college isn't just your classmates—it's your professor, too. How does that change your audience analysis? Your language? Your approach and selection of detail?

> In tone and word choice, this primer is written for undergraduates. How might it be different in word choice and style if professors were the audience?

Writing the Talk

You are giving an oral *presentation*, not an oral chat. While you don't want to be stiff or stuffy, you also don't want to be flip. The optimal tone for a presentation is at once conversational and professional; it should convey to your audience that you are someone worth listening to. Even if the audience consists of your classmates, no "Yo, dudes!" as an opener—just "Thank you." And if everyone doesn't know you, you might give your name ("Hi, I'm Jan . . .").

An oral presentation begins life in one of two ways:

(1) as a previously written paper which you are asked to present as a talk, or

(2) from scratch.

Let's say you are starting your talk from scratch:

"Should I write out an entire draft of my talk?"

There are two ways of answering this question . . .

11% of people in the world are left-handed.

Left Handers' Day is August 13.

When you receive your diploma, shake with the right hand while receiving your certificate with the left.

ON THE ONE HAND If you recall **Rule #3** (Be prepared!), you should know your talk so well that you can reduce it to a few cue words on index cards. You'll refer to these key phrases and concepts if you get nervous or lose your place.

ON THE OTHER HAND There is a good argument for drafting a complete text. The very physical and mental act of writing, as one author on presentations, Charles McConnell, notes, "forces thorough organization and fixes many remarks in the speaker's mind" (74). *Of course, once you have written the text, you can condense it to notes or highlight key phrases and headings.*

As you write the talk, remember to keep it simple **(Rule #1)**:

Use ordinary words

Keep sentences short

AVOID: jargon, abbreviations, sexist language

 See pp. 26-27 for "Words and Phrases to Avoid"

If you have a written version of your talk, rather than note cards, use short paragraphs like the ones in this primer. Type subheads in **bold** and key phrases in **CAPITAL LETTERS**. These features make the text easier to scan and help you keep your place.

A NOTE ON NOTES: if you use cards, number them in sequence so you don't skip any and can keep your cool if they drop.

How do I start?

Get your topic and fundamental message in early.
You can do this in one of two ways:

> **Directly** ("Today I am going to talk about how Abraham Lincoln, a minor candidate in the 1860 presidential election, won the Republican nomination"), or

> **Indirectly**, getting the audience's attention with an interesting story or unexpected fact ("Did you know that in the year Abraham Lincoln was elected, William Seward, not Lincoln, was favored for the Republican Party nomination? How did Lincoln win? That question is the topic of my talk").

Building Your Message: Aristotle's Essential Strategies

The Greek philosopher Aristotle had the brilliant insight 2,500 years ago that every speech, no matter its topic, is woven of three persuasion strategies: **Logos**, **Pathos**, and **Ethos**.

Attend to each as you write and deliver your talk.

LOGOS: Arguments that persuade through **reason and facts**—logic, evidence, statistics.

PATHOS: Words, anecdotes, and evocative descriptions that trigger **emotions** in the audience—anger, fear, grief, pride, etc.

ETHOS: Your **credibility** as a speaker, expressed via your demeanor, voice, language, and dress. It means dress shoes to speak at church—and Vans for your college hip-hop crew talk.

Signposts

Unlike people reading a paper, your listeners only have their ears to follow you (p. 3). They cannot check the text or peek ahead for what's next.

"Signposts" are brief phrases that call attention to key ideas and mark the progress of your talk, summarizing where you have been and pointing the way ahead.

"I want to make three points about good speechwriting . . ."

"My second point is . . ."

"In conclusion . . ."

Internal previews
("Today we'll discover why bread gets stale.
First, we'll . . .Then we'll . . .")

Internal summaries
("Now that we've reviewed the history
of comic books before Superman . . .")

Questions can be signposts:
"Did you know that Dorothy's ruby red slippers were silver in all of the Oz books?"

This question signals: "This is important."

Signposts such as "Finally," or "Equally important," are verbal flashing alerts to your takeaway. For example:
"That's what I want to focus on today: The responsibility each of you has for your education."—*President Barack Obama, September 8, 2009.*

Your audience needs signposts:
Signposts are the Google Maps directions of the spoken word.

How long should my talk be?

Keep it concise. In one study, Stuart and Rutherford found that medical students' concentration during a lecture declines after 10 to 15 minutes (515).

One minute of reading time equals about 150 words (about two-thirds of a double-spaced 11 or 12 pt. page of text).

Humor?

A witty phrase or a pungent observation can help speakers connect with their audience. But be careful. Trying to be funny and falling flat is awkward for you and your listeners.

What about a conclusion?

Have one. It's your last chance to nail your takeaway message.

But keep it brief. Do not add new information. *(Sorry: too late.)*

As in any good performance, leave your audience not needing more, but wanting more.

The "close," as the conclusion of a talk is called, has a good chance of being what your audience remembers most. End strong—with a pithy, relevant quote, anecdote, or reprise of your thesis or message.

Avoiding Plagiarism

It is illegal for anyone to violate any of the rights provided by the copyright law to the owner of copyright.

—U.S. Copyright Office

You already know it's **WRONG** to take someone else's writing or ideas and pass them off as your own.

But you may not know that plagiarism is also a violation of **federal law**, specifically, title 17, U.S. Code.

 "Plagiarism" is from the Latin word "plagium." In Roman law, this was the stealing of a slave or child—taking something owned or dearly beloved by another (Green 169).

Whether it is a wholesale cut-and-paste or a slight word rearrangement, it's unethical and it's illegal. And you know it gets you in a world of trouble with your school—especially so in an age of Googling and originality-checking software.

Be safe, not *sorry*: Credit your source.

Be sure to credit anything you mention that is not common knowledge. *("The Beatles were a British rock band" is common knowledge, and requires no citation.)*

> How? See "Documenting Sources," below.

Always **give credit even when paraphrasing** *(putting a source's ideas in your own words).* Err on the safe side: cite!

THE PLAGIARISM IRONY:
You need your expert sources to establish your credibility. Why, then, would you disguise their words as yours?

How Do You Document Sources?

Whatever your mode of communicating—a paper, a speech, a video—you need to document what you say so you are believable (see Aristotle on ethos, p. 14).

But remember: In a speech, you can't provide a long citation for every source, the way you would in the Works Cited page in a research paper. If you did, you would break the flow of your presentation. *What to do?*

KEEP IT SIMPLE.

Add a brief credibility phrase that telegraphs to your audience the expert source of your fact or quote:

> "A **Defense Department** troop estimate released last fall indicated that . . ."

> "In a public lecture delivered in March 2012, Ian Hough, a **professor of economics** at the University of London, argued that . . ."

> "According to a June 24, 2013, **Gallup poll** on campaign finance reform, 79% of respondents would limit fund-raising . . ."

Respected authorities gain your listeners' trust.
Be sure to mention:

> The **type** of source you are citing (a journal, magazine, book, personal interview, documentary, official agency, etc.)

> The **date** of this material

Ask yourself: "*What brief phrases will help this audience accept the authority of this information?*"

III. Presenting the Talk

Remember Rule #3: Be prepared.

Practice, practice, practice

Honest, there is no substitute. The more you are at home with your talk, the more relaxed and energized you'll be presenting it.

> **ALWAYS** practice OUT LOUD—to a mirror, to a roommate, to yourself as you walk around campus. Pretending to talk in your mind is not the same!
>
> Practice against the clock.
>
> Particularly practice the introduction, so you start strong (this will also calm any nerves).

When you are well practiced, you will be less tempted to read the text and more likely to speak directly to your listeners.

LOOK at your audience. *Eyeball-to-eyeball contact.*

Narrow
+ FOCUSED
+ *Intriguing*
= **Manageable, On-Target, and Memorable**

Use Your Voice

In a paper, you can use underlining, bold, and italics to help make your points. In your talk? Reinforce your meaning, and keep your audience's attention, by:

Raising and lowering the volume and pitch of your voice.

Pausing for emphasis.

In other words: *Don't speak in a monotone.*

As you deliver your talk:

Project to the back of the room.

Enunciate the "ending" consonants, the T's, K's, N's, etc.

S-l-oooooooo-w d-o-w-n. Do not speak faster than **140 words** a minute (Bernhardt and Fischer 318).

What about Stage Fright?

It may not help you to hear that feeling nervous is perfectly normal (it even happens to the blithe and the poker-faced). But it's true.

Nerves mean you care and you've worked hard.
But that pat on the back only goes so far.

A Broadway tip: "If you are nervous before the show, you'll do a good job."

Some tips for calming nerves:

Breathe deep: Breathe in and then out for twice as long (Beagrie and Thacker 27).

Focus on your message and communicating it to your audience.

Remember that you'll probably feel better as soon as you get going.

Rehearse!

**Are you a natural gesturer? Good (but don't overdo it).
No? That's o.k. Be yourself.**

What to do with your HANDS? Great question.

Hold something while you talk: your notes, your glasses, a pencil.

FINAL TIPS:

Do get a good night's sleep. (Sorry, but it works wonders.)

Do warm up your voice by singing a happy, energetic

LA, LA, LA, **LA, LA**, LA, LA, LA, LAaaaaaaa!

And smile.

What about Visual Aids?

Use visual aids only if, in fact, they will aid visually.

Maybe it's a simple, unambiguous graph that illustrates child malnutrition in Cleveland . . . or a child's threadbare sneaker that brings to life what it is to be poor.

Or photos, drawings, slides, or short videos from YouTube that illustrate the people, places, or theme of your talk.

Or—a taste-test aid—handing out chocolates, as one speaker on quality control did, asking his audience their opinion of the quality of the candy (Hadfield-Law 1210).

If a PowerPoint or a bobble-head doll helps get your point across— great. If not, why bother?

Charts and Graphs

If you want to show your audience a chart or graph to make a point, be sure:

It is visually simple.

It presents *one idea simply*.

As you prepare a chart or graph:

Make sure it is **READABLE** at a distance. If you can read your illustration on your computer from 5 feet away, your audience will be able to read it when you project it during your talk.

Write a headline that **clearly** states what the illustration is intended to show. *(For the graph below, "Attention by Time" would be a puzzling headline.)*

Here's how the Pew Internet & American Life Project answered the question "How often do teens send and receive text messages?"

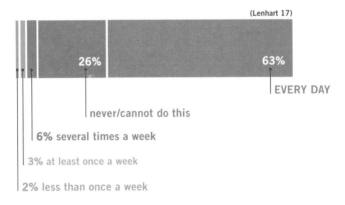

(Lenhart 17)

26%

63%

EVERY DAY

never/cannot do this

6% several times a week

3% at least once a week

2% less than once a week

QUICK!

What's this chart's takeaway message?
(*Easy*—because the answer pops out visually.)

As you present your talk:

    Explain the illustration's relevance to your topic.

    Never read the slide (it's safe to assume your audience can read).

    Never turn your back to your audience to face the slide.

Here are a few basic rules for PowerPoint slides:

The key is ease of reading or scanning (see Rule #1). Therefore:

1. Colors

Keep a strong contrast between background and text (e.g., dark blue on white) so slides can be read from the back of the room. No yellow, unless invisible ink is key to your talk.

**Wheel of
Good/Bad Contrast**

2. BIG Fonts

size 34 – 40 *(like this)* for the main heading and

28 – 32 *(and this)* for text.

3. "The Rule of Six"

A maximum of six lines per slide and six words per line.

Hexakosioihexekontahexaphobia
Fear of the number 666

4. Keep the number of text-only slides to a minimum.

5. Avoid reading your slides. (Boring.)

6. Give only one key detail in each slide.
(Expand with your spoken comments.)

A visual aid checklist (Bernhardt and Fischer 318):

Is it essential?

Is it simple?

Is it large enough?

Recipe for a great speech...

1 part Simplicity

2 parts Repetition

1 part Preparation

a pinch of smiling, confidence, and fun!

Final Reminders

KNOW YOUR MESSAGE

NAIL YOUR TAKEAWAY

KEEP IT SIMPLE

KNOW YOUR AUDIENCE

BREATHE!

DON'T READ

MAINTAIN EYE CONTACT

HAVE A CONCLUSION

HAVE FUN

When you finish your conclusion, say,

1. **"Thank you."**
2. "I'll be glad to answer any questions."
3. Say **"Thank you"** again before you sit down.

Words and Phrases to Avoid (or Use Sparingly)

To Dialogue

synergies

In the final analysis

THE FACT THAT

BANDWIDTH

Um, er, uh, you know, like

strategic

LITERALLY

IT IS WHAT IT IS

folks

Due to the **fact** that

TOTALLY

I'll be honest with you

#$*%@!

Cutting edge/Leading edge/World class/State-of-the-a

24/7

The fact of the matter is

BOGGLES THE MIND

TOUCH BASE

It goes without saying/Needless to say

&*#!

At the present time

AWESOME

Prioritize

CLEARLY

To be honest/to be honest with you/to be perfectly honest

With all due respect

THINKING OUTSIDE THE BOX

To Interface

At the end of the day

BASICALLY

PARADIGM

The truth of the matter is

$^#!*

It was found that (passive)

No word or phrase is completely off-limits, depending on the speech setting, your style, and your specific meaning. In addition, some expressions work well in speaking but not in writing, or vice versa.

Limit your use of common words and phrases that are:
- **Too informal** for most talks (awesome, boggles)
- **Meaningless** (It is what it is, the fact that, you know)
- **Imprecise** (strategic, synergies)
- **Wordy** (at the present time, I'll be honest with you)
- **Overused** or are otherwise off-putting (synergies, to dialogue)

An Example of a Rubric for Evaluating Oral Presentations

CODE
✓+ ⇨ criteria met at a high level :D
✓ ⇨ criteria met :)
✓− ⇨ more work needed :(

	MEASURES	circle one	COMMENTS
CRITERIA: CONTENT	Good opening: Makes clear what the talk is about, why topic is important and/or worth listening to.	✓− ✓ ✓+	
	Good conclusion: Ends with a summary of key points *(for long talks)* and/or with a quote or story or anecdote to illustrate the main idea.	✓− ✓ ✓+	
	Argument makes sense, the ideas flow logically and coherently, with good segues, sources of evidence cited.	✓− ✓ ✓+	
	Information is interesting. Ideas are presented with examples, stories and anecdotes to clarify points.	✓− ✓ ✓+	
CRITERIA: CLARITY	Words enunciated clearly, not mumbled, with effective pauses.	✓− ✓ ✓+	
	Uses appropriate and vivid language, defines key terms, announces transitions from section to section. Spoken loud enough to be heard at the back.	✓− ✓ ✓+	
	Talk is paced well. Ends calmly and is not rushed.	✓− ✓ ✓+	
CRITERIA: NON-VERBAL	Good eye contact with audience.	✓− ✓ ✓+	
	Engaging manner *(smiles, hand gestures, no gang signs)*.	✓− ✓ ✓+	
	No distracting mannerisms *(patting hair, jangling coins in pocket, too many hand gestures)*.	✓− ✓ ✓+	
	Good use of audio-visual aids *(if applicable)* that keep pace with talk, not too cluttered, do not distract from spoken words.	✓− ✓ ✓+	

Source: Mano Singham, Director of the University Center for Innovation in Teaching and Education (UCITE), Case Western Reserve University (2007).